663

D1826880

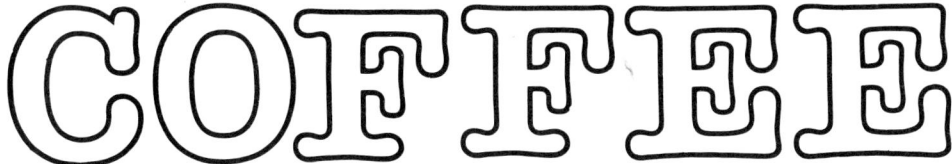

COFFEE

Rhoda Nottridge

Illustrations by John Yates

Wayland

Food

Apples	Herbs and spices
Beans and pulses	Meat
Bread	Milk
Butter	Pasta
Cakes and biscuits	Potatoes
Cheese	Rice
Citrus fruit	Sugar
Coffee	Tea
Eggs	Vegetables
Fish	

All words that appear in **bold** are explained in the glossary on page 30.

Editor: Kevin Rasher.

First published in 1990 by Wayland (Publishers) Limited 61 Western Road, Hove, East Sussex BN3 1JD, England.

British Library Cataloguing in Publication Data
Coffee
  1. Coffee
  I. Title   II. Series
  641.3373

ISBN 0 7502 0045 6

Typeset by Kalligraphic Design Ltd., Horley, Surrey.
Printed in Italy by G. Canale & C.S.p.A., Turin.
Bound by Casterman S.A., Belgium.

Contents

The coffee story

Coffee is one of the world's most popular drinks. It is made from a type of bean which is found inside the bright red fruit of the coffee tree.

How did people first discover that hidden inside the fruit was a bean that could be made into a delicious drink?

The story is told of a goatherder called Kaldi who lived in Ethiopia in Africa, around AD 300.

Coffee trees growing on a hillside in north Yemen.

One day, Kaldi's goats became very lively after feeding on the berries of a coffee tree. Even the oldest goats appeared almost to dance about.

Kaldi took some of the berries to a nearby monastery. The monks threw the beans which they found inside the berries into some boiling water. Later, they sampled the pleasant smelling brew. It tasted wonderful! It made the monks feel lively too, and from then on they drank it before their midnight prayers in order to keep awake.

5

Growing coffee

Coffee trees grow in warm, wet **climates**. Young coffee trees are given special care and watered regularly. As they grow, they are **pruned** so that they are bushy. They are kept at a height of no more than 3 m, to make it easy to pick the fruit.

The trees produce pretty yellow, pink or white flowers. About eight months after the flowers have blossomed, the fruit appear. The fruit are

Planting

Watering

green at first, and it takes about six months for them to ripen to bright red. They are called cherries because of their appearance.

Inside the skin of the coffee cherry there are two green beans, covered in a fine skin and a **pulp** to protect them. It is these little beans that we use to make coffee. But a lot has to happen to them before we can drink them as coffee. Firstly, the ripe cherries are picked by hand or shaken on to a cloth below the trees. Sometimes a machine is used to do this.

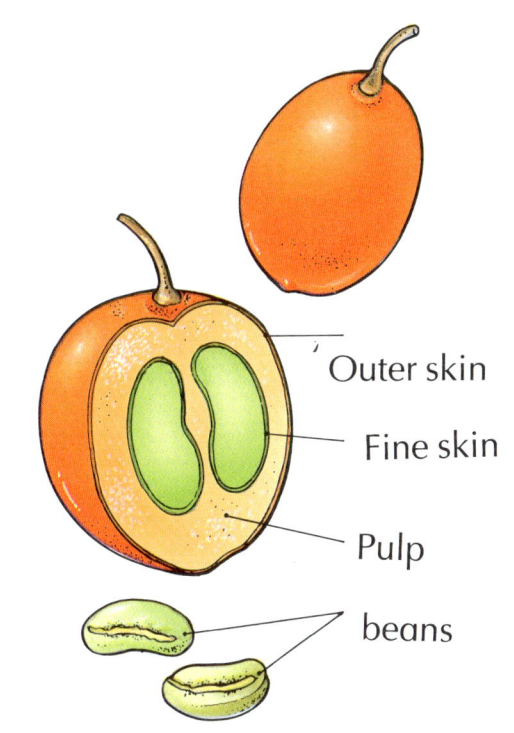

Outer skin

Fine skin

Pulp

beans

Pruning

Picking

7

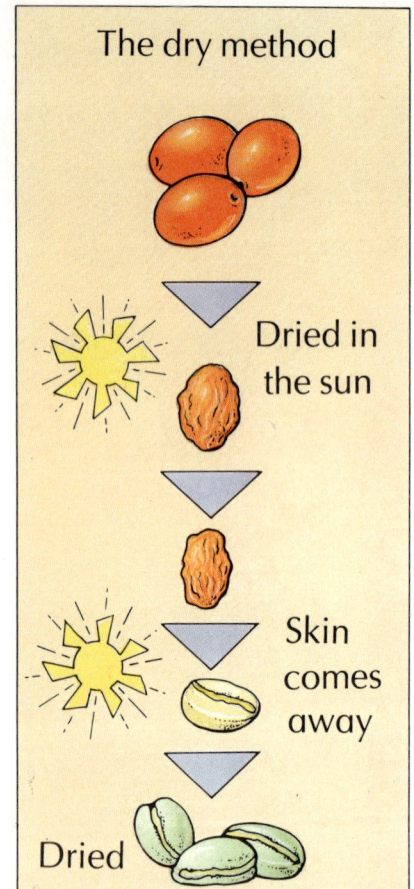

The dry method

Dried in the sun

Skin comes away

Dried

Right *Drying coffee beans in Colombia.*

8

The coffee bean

When the coffee cherries have been gathered, the green beans are taken out of the pulp and skins of the cherries by either the 'dry' or the 'wet' method.

If the cherries are being dried, they are spread out on mats or drying racks in the sun. For two or three weeks they are **raked** over each day. As the cherries dry out, the pulp and skin begin to come away from the beans. The cherries are then put

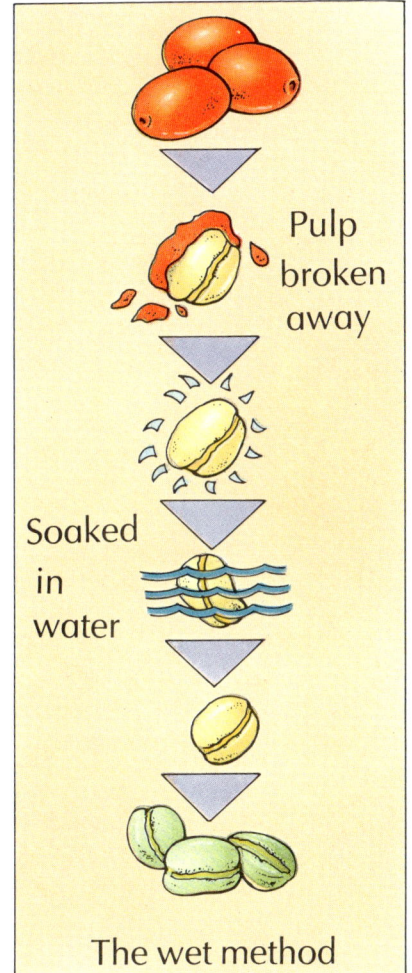

Pulp broken away

Soaked in water

The wet method

into machines to separate the beans completely.

To get to the beans using the wet method, the pulp is broken away by a machine called a pulper. The beans are then soaked in water and dried in the sun or by hot-air machines.

Lastly, they go through a machine which gets rid of the thin skin around the beans. This machine also **grades** the beans.

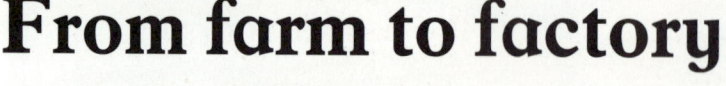

From farm to factory

The clean, graded beans are packed into sacks on the farms where they have been grown. They are then taken to the coffee factory.

Coffee beans have different flavours, depending on where they are grown. The first process in making good coffee at the factory is **blending** the different types of beans from

Above The roasted beans are now ready for grinding.

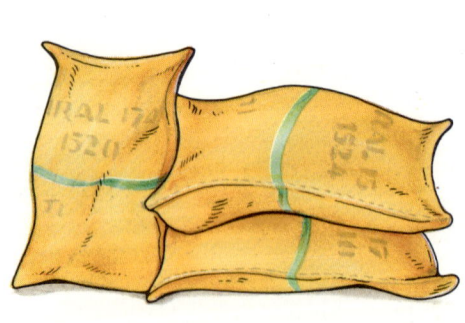

Blending

different farms to give the best flavours and smells.

The green beans are then **roasted** at the factory until they are brown and have nearly doubled in size. The high temperatures bring out the beans' natural oils and let out the smell we expect from coffee.

After roasting, the beans are cooled quickly. Unless the beans are to be sold as they are, they have to be ground and packed, ready for use in a variety of coffee-making machines.

Below This is what happens to the coffee beans at the factory.

Roasting

Cooling

Roasted beans ready for grinding

The taste of coffee

Grinding coffee by hand.

Roasted coffee beans are hard, so the beans have to be ground before the coffee can be brewed with water. Some people like to grind the beans themselves at home. Usually they are ground at the factory.

As soon as the coffee has been ground, it has to be packed in airtight containers. If the coffee is left out in the air its smell and taste will disappear.

Right *This shop sells whole, roasted coffee beans.*

Left This Bedouin is pounding coffee beans into a powder.

Expresso pot

Drip pot

Turkish pot

Plunger pot

Jug

There are many ways of brewing coffee. It can be brewed using jugs, percolators, plunger pots, drip pots and expresso machines. The type of coffee people choose also varies. So does the way it is ground. People buy coffee that has been ground either coarsely or finely, depending on how they like to brew their coffee.

13

Instant coffee

1. One teaspoon of coffee

2. Add hot water

3. Stir well

4. Add milk or cream

One kind of coffee which is very popular today is instant or **soluble** coffee. Instead of pouring water through the ground coffee, this type of coffee is dissolved in hot water. It is ideal for making a quick cup of coffee.

To **manufacture** instant coffee, the beans are first roasted and ground. The coffee is then brewed in hot water in huge tanks, which are sometimes taller than a house. The water in the brew is **evaporated** off in a hot-air drying machine, leaving only the coffee **granules**. They can be drunk when they have been mixed with hot water in a cup.

The most modern method of manufacturing instant coffee is called freeze-drying. The liquid brew is frozen and then dried. This allows even more of the flavour to be kept in the coffee.

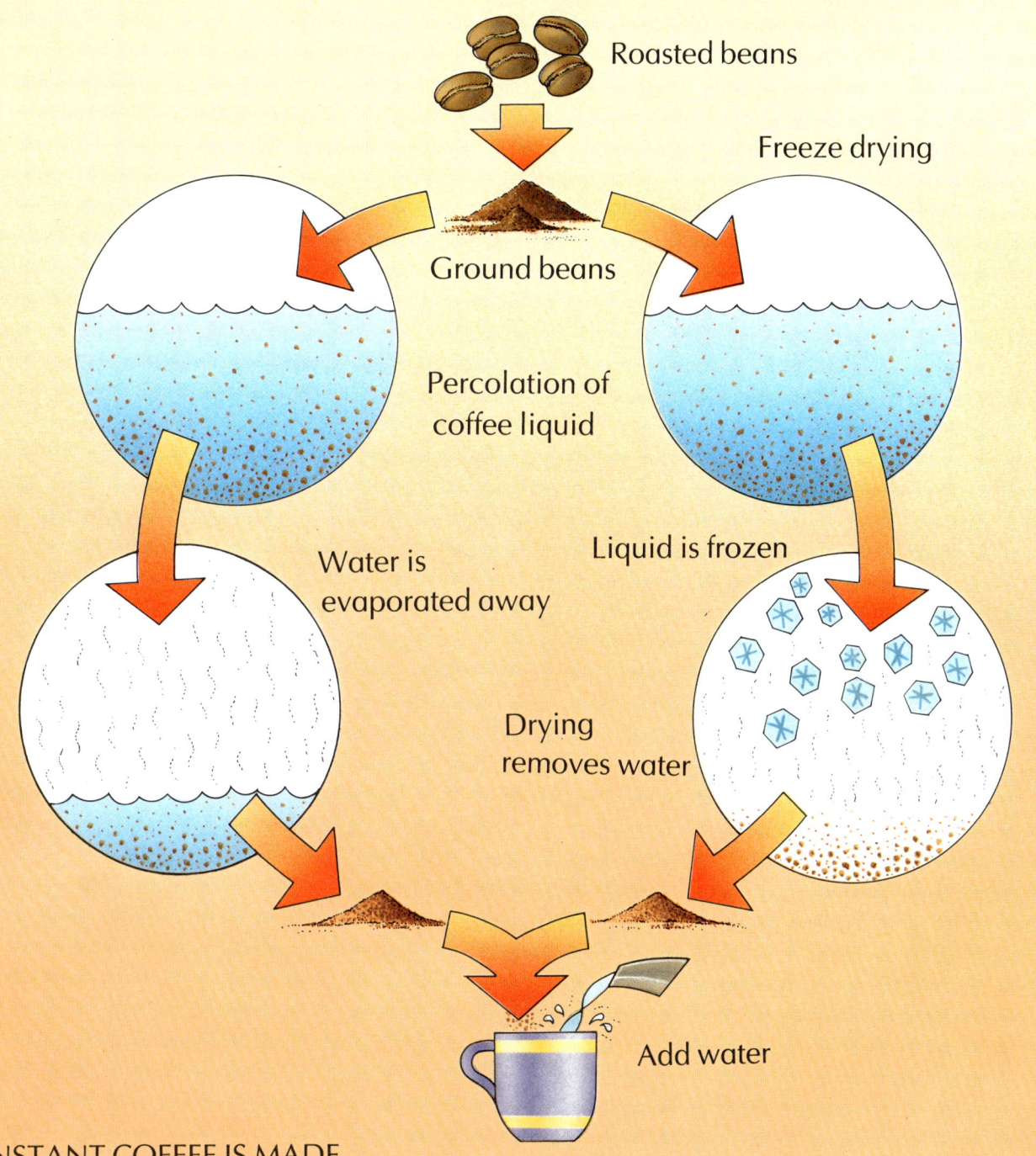

Roasted beans

Freeze drying

Ground beans

Percolation of
coffee liquid

Water is
evaporated away

Liquid is frozen

Drying
removes water

Add water

15

The history of coffee

The goatherder Kaldi could never have imagined how popular the beans that made his goats dance would become. Coffee drinking spread quickly from Africa to Arabia. It was particularly liked by Muslims and became known as 'the wine of Arabia'.

Coffee was brought to Italy in the seventeenth century, and soon there were many coffee

A coffee house in Constantinople (now Istanbul in modern Turkey). Coffee was once known as the 'wine of Arabia'.

16

Left A rowdy scene in an English coffee house in 1813.

Below Drinking coffee in southern USA.

houses throughout Europe. In Britain they were called 'penny universities'. This was because they cost a penny to get into and you could sit and listen to **scholars** talking to each other as they drank their coffee.

Coffee was later taken from Britain to the USA, which was a British **colony** at the time. It did not become really popular in the USA until 1773, when Americans complained about the British **tax** on tea sold in America. To show how unhappy they were with the tax, the Americans stopped drinking tea and turned to coffee instead. Ever since that time, coffee has been more popular than tea in the USA.

The growth of the coffee trade

In the early eighteenth century, Arabia produced nearly all the world's coffee. Then Holland started to grow coffee in its colonies in Asia and South America. It soon became a very **profitable** crop for the Dutch.

In 1714, the mayor of Amsterdam kindly offered King Louis XIV of France a young coffee tree for his famous garden. A naval officer

De Clieu waters his tiny coffee plant on the long voyage across the Atlantic.

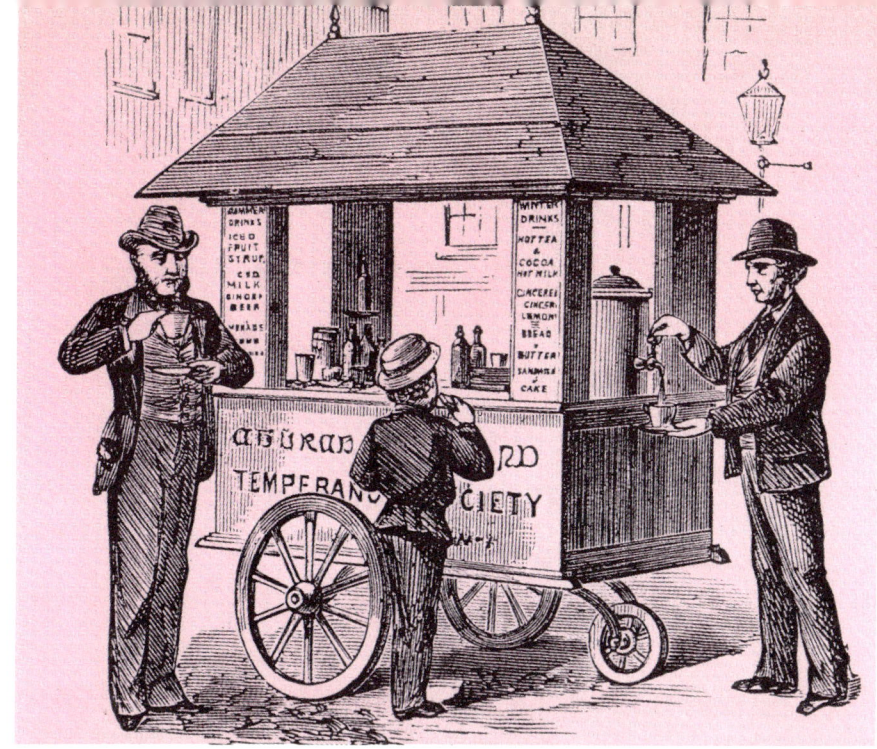

named De Clieu took a tiny cutting from the tree on a sea voyage across the Atlantic Ocean to the Caribbean Islands. The ship was attacked by pirates and ran into a terrible storm. De Clieu kept the coffee plant alive with his own precious drinking water.

His care was not wasted, and the plant grew successfully on the island of Martinique. By 1777, the island had around 18 million coffee trees.

The French and Dutch jealously guarded their coffee plants. They did not want other countries to share the wealth they were gaining from selling their coffee beans.

There is an interesting story of how in 1727 coffee first reached Brazil. A young Brazilian soldier in Guyana was handed a bouquet of flowers as a leaving present. The wife of the French governor of Guyana had fallen in love

A French coffee plantation in the nineteenth century. Workers had to work hard for little money.

Coffee pickers on their way to work in Thailand.

Below *The little coffee bush was hidden among the soldier's flowers.*

with the young man. Inside the bouquet that she gave him was a small coffee plant, hidden among the flowers. The young man took the bush with him to Brazil. Today, Brazil is the world's largest coffee producer.

Coffee is now grown in more than 40 countries. It is one of the world's most important crops and over 20 million people work in the coffee **industry**.

21

Coffee and health

Many years ago, coffee was drunk by rich people as a medicine. But for centuries there have been people who have said that coffee is bad for a person's health.

Coffee contains **caffeine**, which can make people feel more lively and awake. Too much caffeine can stop a person sleeping well. For this

Doctors now know that drinking too much coffee each day can cause health problems.

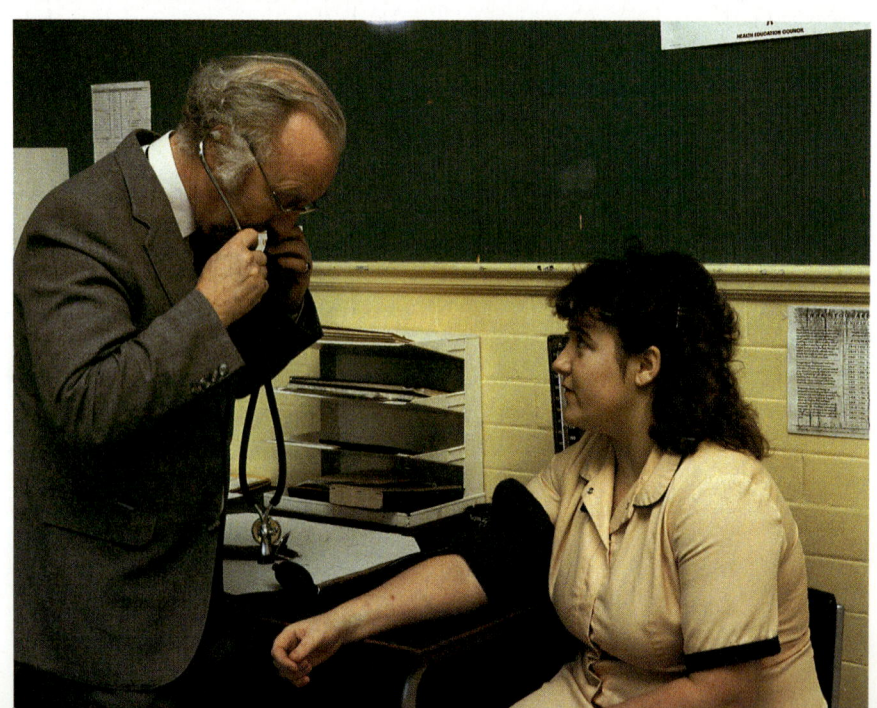

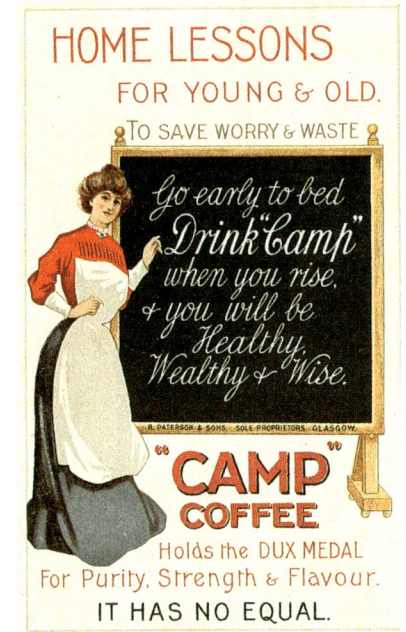

HOME LESSONS
FOR YOUNG & OLD.
TO SAVE WORRY & WASTE
Go early to bed Drink "Camp" when you rise, & you will be Healthy, Wealthy & Wise.
R. PATERSON & SONS. SOLE PROPRIETORS. GLASGOW.
"CAMP" COFFEE
Holds the DUX MEDAL
For Purity, Strength & Flavour.
IT HAS NO EQUAL.

reason, it is not a good drink for children, as they can be affected by the caffeine more than adults.

Many people who like the flavour of coffee, but do not want to drink the caffeine, buy decaffeinated coffee. In factories that manufacture decaffeinated coffee, the beans are soaked in a **chemical** that dissolves the caffeine. The chemical is steamed off the beans. The beans are then roasted like ordinary coffee beans. It tastes just as good!

The international drink

Coffee is drunk in many different ways around the world. In some parts of Europe and in the USA, people usually **filter** their coffee to get rid of the grounds. British and American people like finely ground, lightly roasted coffee with milk or cream. In South America, Spain and Italy, people prefer highly roasted, strong coffee which they drink out of very small cups.

Many Italians drink cappuccino, a frothy coffee drink made with milk and sprinkled with chocolate.

Left Enjoying coffee in Saudi Arabia.

Below A Norwegian soldier drinking coffee to keep warm.

In some countries, coffee is drunk in ways which have not changed for hundreds of years. The beans are well roasted and the coffee is ground into a very fine powder. After brewing, the coffee is poured into cups with the grounds still in the liquid. The grounds sink to the bottom of the cup. The secret of drinking this type of coffee is to sip it carefully. If it is gulped down, the drinker will get a mouthful of coffee grounds, which is like having sand in your mouth. This rich, strong drink is called Greek or Turkish coffee.

Coffee is often used as a flavouring in food. Here are some recipes using coffee for you to try.

Coffee ice-cream soda

You will need:
1 bottle of soda water
400ml coffee
150ml single cream
1 block of ice-cream
sugar to taste

2. Stir in 150ml of single cream. Pour the mixture into tall glasses, until they are half full.

1. Make up 400ml of coffee and add a little sugar to taste. Leave it to cool in a fridge.

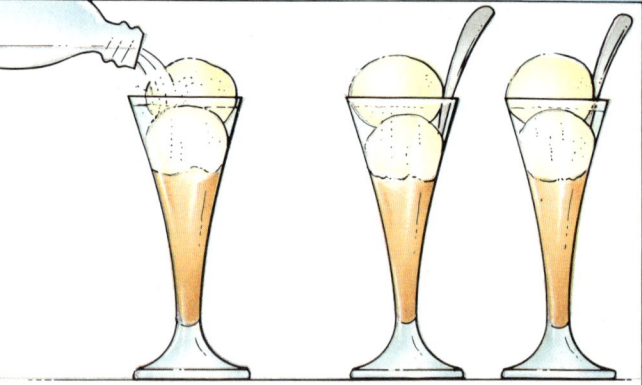

3. Add two scoops of ice-cream to each glass and top up the glasses with soda water, pouring it slowly over the ice-cream. Serve at once.

Coffee and walnut cake

You will need:

2 level teaspoons of instant coffee, dissolved in 1 tablespoon of boiling water, then cooled

2 large eggs

60g chopped walnuts

125g each of soft margarine, caster sugar and self-raising flour

1 level teaspoon of baking powder

2. Put the mixture into a greased baking tin.

1. Put all the ingredients in a large bowl and mix well.

3. Place the baking tin in the oven and bake for 35 minutes at 160°C, 325°F, gas mark 3. Ask an adult to help you remove the cake from the oven.

27

Coffee custard

You will need:
500ml milk
2 teaspoons of instant coffee
3 tablespoons of sugar
4 eggs

2. Stir in the sugar.

1. Mix the coffee with the milk, put in a pan and bring to the boil.

3. Crack one egg into a bowl. Separate the other three yolks from the whites of the eggs, and stir in the yolks.

4. Slowly pour the milk into the bowl and beat it in with the eggs.

6. Put the ramekins together into a larger container and fill the larger container with water, reaching about two-thirds of the way up the sides of the ramekin dishes.

5. Pour into ramekins or other small ovenproof dishes.

7. Bake in the oven at 160°C, 325°F, gas mark 3 for about 45 minutes. They are ready when the mixture is set. Ask an adult to help you remove them from the oven.

Glossary

Blend To mix flavours or smells together smoothly, to produce a new flavour or smell.

Caffeine A stimulating substance found in coffee, which makes you feel more lively.

Chemical A substance obtained by chemistry.

Climates The normal weather conditions in particular areas.

Colony A country which is ruled by another country.

Evaporated When liquid is lost by heating it so that it turns into vapour.

Filter To pass a liquid through a kind of netting which catches the solids and allows only the liquid to pass through it.

Grade Select something according to how good it is.

Granules Small, grain-like pieces.

Industry The making, producing or processing in factories of things for sale.

Manufacture To make something with machines.

Profitable A thing is profitable if it can be sold for more money than it cost to buy, make or grow.

Pulp A woody fibre that protects the bean or seed inside it.

Pruned When the branches of a tree or bush have been cut to leave the remaining branches healthier and give the tree a better shape.

Raked Pulled over with a rake.

Roasted Cooked at a high temperature, which usually browns the food.

Scholars People who study and read a lot.

Soluble A substance is soluble if it can be dissolved in another substance.

Tax Money that people pay to the government.

Books to read

A Cup of Coffee by Julian Fox (Wayland, 1983)

Coffee by V. Pitt (Franklin Watts, 1982)

Coffee by M. Smith (Ladybird, 1977)

Chocolate, Tea and Coffee by C. de Sairigne (Moonlight Publishing, 1986)

The Coffee Story, available from the London Coffee Information Centre, 22 Berners Street, London W1P 4DD.

Index

Picture acknowledgements

The photographs in this book were provided by: Mary Evans Picture Library 17 (top), 18, 20, 23 (bottom); Hutchison Library 5; International Coffee Organization 9, 17 (bottom), 21; Christine Osborne/Middle East Pictures 4, 13, 25 (top); Ann Ronan 16, 19 (both); Peter Stiles COVER; Topham Picture Library 12, 22, 24; Wayland Picture Library 25 (bottom); ZEFA 8, 10, 23 (top).